I0439865

Fourth State of the Union Address

JAMES BUCHANAN

Published in 1860

TABLE OF CONTENTS

FOURTH STATE OF THE UNION ADDRESS

FOURTH STATE OF THE UNION ADDRESS

Fellow-Citizens of the Senate and House of Representatives:

Throughout the year since our last meeting the country has been eminently prosperous in all its material interests. The general health has been excellent, our harvests have been abundant, and plenty smiles throughout the laud. Our commerce and manufactures have been prosecuted with energy and industry, and have yielded fair and ample returns. In short, no nation in the tide of time has ever presented a spectacle of greater material prosperity than we have done until within a very recent period.

Why is it, then, that discontent now so extensively prevails, and the Union of the States, which is the source of all these blessings, is threatened with destruction?

The long-continued and intemperate interference of the Northern people with the question of slavery in the Southern States has at length produced its natural effects. The different sections of the Union are now arrayed against each other, and the time has arrived, so much dreaded by the Father of his Country, when hostile geographical parties have been formed.

I have long foreseen and often forewarned my countrymen of the now impending danger. This does not proceed solely from the claim on the part of Congress or the Territorial legislatures to exclude slavery from the Territories, nor from the efforts of different States to defeat the execution of the fugitive-slave law. All or any of these evils might have been endured by the South without danger to the Union (as others have been) in the hope that time and reflection might apply the remedy. The immediate peril arises not so much from these causes as from the fact that the incessant and violent agitation of the slavery question throughout the North for the last quarter of a century has at length produced its malign influence on the slaves and inspired them with vague notions of freedom. Hence a sense of security no longer exists around the family altar. This feeling of peace at home has given place to apprehensions of servile insurrections. Many a matron throughout the South retires at night in dread of what may befall herself and children before the morning. Should this apprehension of domestic danger, whether real or imaginary, extend and intensify itself until it shall pervade the masses of the Southern people, then disunion will become inevitable. Self-preservation is the first law of nature, and has been implanted in the heart of man by his Creator for the wisest purpose; and no political union, however fraught with blessings and benefits in all other respects, can long continue if the necessary consequence be to render the homes and the firesides of nearly half the parties to it habitually and hopelessly insecure. Sooner or later the bonds of such a union must be severed. It is my conviction that this fatal period has not yet arrived, and my prayer to God is that He would preserve the Constitution and the Union throughout all generations.

But let us take warning in time and remove the cause of danger. It can not be denied that for five and twenty years the agitation at the North against slavery has been incessant. In 1835 pictorial handbills and inflammatory appeals were circulated extensively throughout the South of a character to excite the passions of the slaves, and, in the language of General Jackson, "to stimulate them to insurrection and produce all the horrors of a servile war." This agitation has ever since been continued by the public press, by the proceedings of State and county conventions and by abolition sermons and lectures. The time of Congress has been occupied in violent speeches on this never-ending subject, and appeals, in pamphlet and other forms, indorsed by distinguished names, have been sent forth from this central point and spread broadcast over the Union.

How easy would it be for the American people to settle the slavery question forever and to restore peace and harmony to this distracted country! They, and they alone, can do it. All that is necessary to accomplish the object, and all for which the slave States have ever contended, is to be let alone and permitted to manage their domestic institutions in their own way. As sovereign States, they, and they alone, are responsible before God and the world for the slavery existing among them. For this the people of the North are not more responsible and have no more right to interfere than with similar institutions in Russia or in Brazil.

Upon their good sense and patriotic forbearance I confess I still greatly rely. Without their aid it is beyond the power of any President, no matter what may be his own political proclivities, to restore peace and harmony among the States. Wisely limited and restrained as is his power under our

Constitution and laws, he alone can accomplish but little for good or for evil on such a momentous question.

And this brings me to observe that the election of any one of our fellow-citizens to the office of President does not of itself afford just cause for dissolving the Union. This is more especially true if his election has been effected by a mere plurality, and not a majority of the people, and has resulted from transient and temporary causes, which may probably never again occur. In order to justify a resort to revolutionary resistance, the Federal Government must be guilty of "a deliberate, palpable, and dangerous exercise" of powers not granted by the Constitution.

The late Presidential election, however, has been held in strict conformity with its express provisions. How, then, can the result justify a revolution to destroy this very Constitution? Reason, justice, a regard for the Constitution, all require that we shall wait for some overt and dangerous act on the part of the President elect before resorting to such a remedy. It is said, however, that the antecedents of the President-elect have been sufficient to justify the fears of the South that he will attempt to invade their constitutional rights. But are such apprehensions of contingent danger in the future sufficient to justify the immediate destruction of the noblest system of government ever devised by mortals? From the very nature of his office and its high responsibilities he must necessarily be conservative. The stern duty of administering the vast and complicated concerns of this Government affords in itself a guaranty that he will not attempt any violation of a clear constitutional right.

After all, he is no more than the chief executive officer of the Government. His province is not to make but to execute the laws. And it is a remarkable fact in our history that, notwithstanding the repeated efforts of the antislavery party, no single act has ever passed Congress, unless we may possibly except the Missouri compromise, impairing in the slightest degree the rights of the South to their property in slaves; and it may also be observed, judging from present indications, that no probability exists of the passage of such an act by a majority of both Houses, either in the present or the next Congress. Surely under these circumstances we ought to be restrained from present action by the precept of Him who spake as man never spoke, that "sufficient unto the day is the evil thereof." The day of evil may never come unless we shall rashly bring it upon ourselves.

It is alleged as one cause for immediate secession that the Southern States are denied equal rights with the other States in the common Territories. But by what authority are these denied? Not by Congress, which has never passed, and I believe never will pass, any act to exclude slavery from these Territories; and certainly not by the Supreme Court, which has solemnly decided that slaves are property, and, like all other property, their owners have a right to take them into the common Territories and hold them there under the protection of the Constitution.

So far then, as Congress is concerned, the objection is not to anything they have already done, but to what they may do hereafter. It will surely be admitted that this apprehension of future danger is no good reason for an immediate dissolution of the Union. It is true that the Territorial legislature of Kansas, on the 23d February, 1860, passed in great haste an act over the veto of the governor declaring that slavery "is and shall be forever prohibited in this Territory." Such an act, however, plainly violating the rights of property secured by the Constitution, will surely be declared void by the judiciary whenever it shall be presented in a legal form.

Only three days after my inauguration the Supreme Court of the United States solemnly adjudged that this power did not exist in a Territorial legislature. Yet such has been the factious temper of the times that the correctness of this decision has been extensively impugned before the people, and the question has given rise to angry political conflicts throughout the country. Those who have appealed from this judgment of our highest constitutional tribunal to popular assemblies would, if they could, invest a Territorial legislature with power to annul the sacred rights of property. This power Congress is expressly forbidden by the Federal Constitution to exercise. Every State legislature in the Union is forbidden by its own constitution to exercise it. It can not be exercised in any State except by the people in their highest sovereign capacity, when framing or amending their State constitution. In like manner it can only be exercised by the people of a Territory represented in a convention of delegates for the purpose of framing a constitution preparatory to admission as a State into the Union. Then, and not until then, are they invested with power to decide the question whether slavery shall or shall not exist within their limits. This is an act of sovereign authority, and not of subordinate Territorial legislation. Were it otherwise, then indeed would the equality of the States in the Territories be destroyed, and the rights of property in slaves would depend not upon the guaranties of the Constitution, but upon the shifting majorities of an irresponsible Territorial legislature. Such a doctrine, from its intrinsic unsoundness, can not long influence any considerable portion of our people, much less can it afford a good reason for a dissolution of the Union.

The most palpable violations of constitutional duty which have yet been committed consist in the acts of different State legislatures to defeat the execution of the fugitive-slave law. It ought to be remembered, however, that for these acts neither Congress nor any President can justly be held responsible. Having been passed in violation of the Federal Constitution, they are therefore null and void. All the courts, both State and national, before whom the question has arisen have from the beginning declared the fugitive-slave law to be constitutional. The single exception is that of a State court in Wisconsin, and this has not only been reversed by the proper appellate tribunal, but has met with such universal reprobation that there can be no danger from it as a precedent. The validity of this law has been established over and over again by the Supreme Court of the United States with perfect unanimity. It is rounded upon an express provision of the Constitution, requiring that fugitive slaves who escape from service in one State to another shall be "delivered up" to their masters. Without this provision it is a well-known historical fact that the Constitution itself could never have been adopted by the Convention. In one form or other, under the acts of 1793 and 1850, both being substantially the same, the fugitive-slave law has been the law of the land from the days of Washington until the present moment. Here, then, a clear case is presented in which it will be the duty of the next President, as it has been my own, to act with vigor in executing this supreme law against the conflicting enactments of State legislatures. Should he fail in the performance of this high duty, he will then have manifested a disregard of the Constitution and laws, to the great injury of the people of nearly one-half of the States of the Union. But are we to presume in advance that he will thus violate his duty? This would be at war with every principle of justice and of Christian charity. Let us wait for the overt act. The fugitive-slave law has been carried into execution in every contested case since the commencement of the present Administration, though Often, it is to be regretted, with great loss and inconvenience to the master and with considerable expense to the Government. Let us trust that the State legislatures will repeal their unconstitutional and obnoxious enactments. Unless this shall be done without unnecessary delay, it is impossible for any human power to save the Union.

The Southern States, standing on the basis of the Constitution, have right to demand this act of justice from the States of the North. Should it be refused, then the Constitution, to which all the States are parties, will have been willfully violated by one portion of them in a provision essential to the domestic security and happiness of the remainder. In that event the injured States, after having first used all peaceful and constitutional means to obtain redress, would be justified in revolutionary resistance to the Government of the Union.

I have purposely confined my remarks to revolutionary resistance, because it has been claimed within the last few years that any State, whenever this shall be its sovereign will and pleasure, may secede from the Union in accordance with the Constitution and without any violation of the constitutional rights of the other members of the Confederacy; that as each became parties to the Union by the vote of its own people assembled in convention, so any one of them may retire from the Union in a similar manner by the vote of such a convention.

In order to justify secession as a constitutional remedy, it must be on the principle that the Federal Government is a mere voluntary association of States, to be dissolved at pleasure by any one of the contracting parties. If this be so, the Confederacy is a rope of sand, to be penetrated and dissolved by the first adverse wave of public opinion in any of the States. In this manner our thirty-three States may resolve themselves into as many petty, jarring, and hostile republics, each one retiring from the Union without responsibility whenever any sudden excitement might impel them to such a course. By this process a Union might be entirely broken into fragments in a few weeks which cost our forefathers many years of toil, privation, and blood to establish.

Such a principle is wholly inconsistent with the history as well as the character of the Federal Constitution. After it was framed with the greatest deliberation and care it was submitted to conventions of the people of the several States for ratification. Its provisions were discussed at length in these bodies, composed of the first men of the country. Its opponents contended that it conferred powers upon the Federal Government dangerous to the rights of the States, whilst its advocates maintained that under a fair construction of the instrument there was no foundation for such apprehensions. In that mighty struggle between the first intellects of this or any other country it never occurred to any individual, either among its opponents or advocates, to assert or even to intimate that their efforts were all vain labor, because the moment that any State felt herself aggrieved she might secede from the Union. What a crushing argument would this have proved against those who dreaded that the rights of the States would be endangered by the Constitution! The truth is that it was not until many years after the origin of the Federal Government that such a proposition was first advanced. It was then met and refuted by the conclusive arguments of General Jackson, who in his message of the 16th of January, 1833, transmitting the nullifying ordinance of South Carolina to Congress, employs the following language:

The right of the people of a single State to absolve themselves at will and without the consent of the other States from their most solemn obligations, and hazard the liberties and happiness of the millions composing this Union, can not be acknowledged. Such authority is believed to be utterly repugnant both to the principles upon which the General Government is constituted and to the objects which it is expressly formed to attain.

It is not pretended that any clause in the Constitution gives countenance to such a theory. It is altogether rounded upon inference; not from any language contained in the instrument itself, but from the sovereign character of the several States by which it was ratified. But is it beyond the power of a State, like an individual, to yield a portion of its sovereign rights to secure the remainder? In the language of Mr. Madison, who has been called the father of the Constitution-

It was formed by the States; that is, by the people in each of the States acting in their highest sovereign capacity, and formed, consequently, by the same authority which formed the State constitutions. Nor is the Government of the United States, created by the Constitution, less a government, in the strict sense of the term, within the sphere of its powers than the governments created by the constitutions of the States are within their several spheres. It is, like them, organized into legislative, executive, and judiciary departments. It operates, like them directly on persons and things, and, like them, it has at command a physical force for executing the powers committed to it.

It was intended to be perpetual, and not to be annulled at the pleasure of any one of the contracting parties. The old Articles of Confederation were entitled "Articles of Confederation and Perpetual Union between the States," and by the thirteenth article it is expressly declared that "the articles of this Confederation shall be inviolably observed by every State, and the Union shall be perpetual." The preamble to the Constitution of the United States, having express reference to the Articles of Confederation, recites that it was established "in order to form a more perfect union." And yet it is contended that this "more perfect union" does not include the essential attribute of perpetuity.

But that the Union was designed to be perpetual appears conclusively from the nature and extent of the powers conferred by the Constitution on the Federal Government. These powers embrace the very highest attributes of national sovereignty. They place both the sword and the purse under its control. Congress has power to make war and to make peace, to raise and support armies and navies, and to conclude treaties with foreign governments. It is invested with the power to coin money and to regulate the value thereof, and to regulate commerce with foreign nations and among the several States. It is not necessary to enumerate the other high powers which have been conferred upon the Federal Government. In order to carry the enumerated powers into effect, Congress possesses the exclusive right to lay and collect duties on imports, and, in common with the States, to lay and collect all other taxes.

But the Constitution has not only conferred these high powers upon Congress, but it has adopted effectual means to restrain the States from interfering with their exercise. For that purpose it has in strong prohibitory language expressly declared that-

No State shall enter into any treaty, alliance, or confederation; grant letters of marque and reprisal; coin money; emit bills of credit; make anything but gold and silver coin a tender in payment of debts; pass any bill of attainder, ex post facto law, or law impairing the obligation of contracts.

Moreover- No State shall without the consent of the Congress lay any imposts or duties on imports or exports, except what may be absolutely necessary for executing its inspection laws.

And if they exceed this amount the excess shall belong, to the United States. And- No State shall without the consent of Congress lay any duty of tonnage, keep troops or ships of war in time of peace, enter into any agreement or compact with another State or with a foreign power, or engage in war, unless actually invaded or in such imminent danger as will not admit of delay.

In order still further to secure the uninterrupted exercise of these high powers against State interposition, it is provided that- This Constitution and the laws of the United States which shall be made in pursuance thereof, and all treaties made or which shall be made under the authority of the United States, shall be the supreme law of the land, and the judges in every State shall be bound thereby, anything in the constitution or laws of any State to the contrary notwithstanding.

The solemn sanction of religion has been superadded to the obligations of official duty, and all Senators and Representatives of the United States, all members of State legislatures, and all executive and judicial officers, "both of the United States and of the several States, shall be bound by oath or affirmation to support this Constitution."

In order to carry into effect these powers, the Constitution has established a perfect Government in all its forms-legislative, executive, and judicial; and this Government to the extent of its powers acts directly upon the individual citizens of every State, and executes its own decrees by the agency of its own officers. In this respect it differs entirely from the Government under the old Confederation, which was confined to making requisitions on the States in their sovereign character. This left it in the discretion of each whether to obey or to refuse, and they often declined to comply with such requisitions. It thus became necessary for the purpose of removing this barrier and "in order to form a more perfect union" to establish a Government which could act directly upon the people and execute its own laws without the intermediate agency of the States. This has been accomplished by the Constitution of the United States. In short, the Government created by the Constitution, and deriving its authority from the sovereign people of each of the several States, has precisely the same right to exercise its power over the people of all these States in in the enumerated cases that each one of them possesses over subjects not delegated to the United States, but "reserved to the States respectively or to the people."

To the extent of the delegated powers the Constitution of the United States is as much a part of the constitution of each State and is as binding upon its people as though it had been textually inserted therein.

This Government, therefore, is a great and powerful Government, invested with all the attributes of sovereignty over the special subjects to which its authority extends. Its framers never intended to implant in its bosom the seeds of its own destruction, nor were they at its creation guilty of the absurdity of providing for its own dissolution. It was not intended by its framers to be the baseless fabric of a vision, which at the touch of the enchanter would vanish into thin air, but a substantial and mighty fabric, capable of resisting the slow decay of time and of defying the storms of ages. Indeed, well may the jealous patriots of that day have indulged fears that a Government of such high powers might violate the reserved rights of the States, and wisely did they adopt the rule of a strict construction of these powers to prevent the danger. But they did not fear, nor had they any reason to imagine, that the Constitution would ever be so interpreted as to enable any State by her own act, and without the consent of her sister States, to discharge her people from all or any of their federal obligations.

It may be asked, then, Are the people of the States without redress against the tyranny and oppression of the Federal Government? By no means. The right of resistance on the part of the governed against the oppression of their governments can not be denied. It exists independently of all constitutions, and has been exercised at all periods of the world's history. Under it old governments have been destroyed and new ones have taken their place. It is embodied in strong and express language in our own Declaration of Independence. But the distinction must ever be observed that this is revolution against an established government, and not a voluntary secession from it by virtue of an inherent constitutional right. In short, let us look the danger fairly in the face. Secession is neither more nor less than revolution. It may or it may not be a justifiable revolution, but still it is revolution.

What, in the meantime, is the responsibility and true position of the Executive? He is bound by solemn oath, before God and the country, "to take care that the laws be faithfully executed," and from this obligation he can not be absolved by any human power. But what if the performance of this duty, in whole or in part, has been rendered impracticable by events over which he could have exercised no control? Such at the present moment is the case throughout the State of South Carolina so far as the laws of the United States to secure the administration of justice by means of the Federal judiciary are concerned. All the Federal officers within its limits through whose agency alone these laws can be carried into execution have already resigned. We no longer have a district judge, a district attorney, or a marshal in South Carolina. In fact, the whole machinery of the Federal Government necessary for the distribution of remedial justice among the people has been demolished, and it would be difficult, if not impossible, to replace it.

The only acts of Congress on the statute book bearing upon this subject are those of February 28, 1795, and March 3, 1807. These authorize the

President, after he shall have ascertained that the marshal, with his posse comitatus, is unable to execute civil or criminal process in any particular case, to call forth the militia and employ the Army and Navy to aid him in performing this service, having first by proclamation commanded the insurgents "to disperse and retire peaceably to their respective abodes within a limited time" This duty can not by possibility be performed in a State where no judicial authority exists to issue process, and where there is no marshal to execute it, and where, even if there were such an officer, the entire population would constitute one solid combination to resist him.

The bare enumeration of these provisions proves how inadequate they are without further legislation to overcome a united opposition in a single State, not to speak of other States who may place themselves in a similar attitude. Congress alone has power to decide whether the present laws can or can not be amended so as to carry out more effectually the objects of the Constitution.

The same insuperable obstacles do not lie in the way of executing the laws for the collection of the customs. The revenue still continues to be collected as heretofore at the custom-house in Charleston, and should the collector unfortunately resign a successor may be appointed to perform this duty.

Then, in regard to the property of the United States in South Carolina. This has been purchased for a fair equivalent, "by the consent of the legislature of the State," "for the erection of forts, magazines, arsenals," etc., and over these the authority "to exercise exclusive legislation" has been expressly granted by the Constitution to Congress. It is not believed that any attempt will be made to expel the United States from this property by force; but if in this I should prove to be mistaken, the officer in command of the forts has received orders to act strictly on the defensive. In such a contingency the responsibility for consequences would rightfully rest upon the heads of the assailants.

Apart from the execution of the laws, so far as this may be practicable, the Executive has no authority to decide what shall be the relations between the Federal Government and South Carolina. He has been invested with no such discretion. He possesses no power to change the relations heretofore existing between them, much less to acknowledge the independence of that State. This would be to invest a mere executive officer with the power of recognizing the dissolution of the confederacy among our thirty-three sovereign States. It bears no resemblance to the recognition of a foreign de facto government, involving no such responsibility. Any attempt to do this would, on his part, be a naked act of usurpation. It is therefore my duty to submit to Congress the whole question in all its beatings. The course of events is so rapidly hastening forward that the emergency may soon arise when you may be called upon to decide the momentous question whether you possess the power by force of arms to compel a State to remain in the

Union. I should feel myself recreant to my duty were I not to express an opinion on this important subject.

The question fairly stated is, Has the Constitution delegated to Congress the power to coerce a State into submission which is attempting to withdraw or has actually withdrawn from the Confederacy? If answered in the affirmative, it must be on the principle that the power has been conferred upon Congress to declare and to make war against a State. After much serious reflection I have arrived at the conclusion that no such power has been delegated to Congress or to any other department of the Federal Government. It is manifest upon an inspection of the Constitution that this is not among the specific and enumerated powers granted to Congress, and it is equally apparent that its exercise is not "necessary and proper for carrying into execution" any one of these powers. So far from this power having been delegated to Congress, it was expressly refused by the Convention which framed the Constitution.

It appears from the proceedings of that body that on the 31st May, 1787, the clause "authorizing an exertion of the force of the whole against a delinquent State" came up for consideration. Mr. Madison opposed it in a brief but powerful speech, from which I shall extract but a single sentence. He observed:

The use of force against a State would look more like a declaration of war than an infliction of punishment, and would probably be considered by the party attacked as a dissolution of all previous compacts by which it might be bound.

Upon his motion the clause was unanimously postponed, and was never, I believe, again presented. Soon afterwards, on the 8th June, 1787, when incidentally adverting to the subject, he said: "Any government for the United States formed on the supposed practicability of using force against the unconstitutional proceedings of the States would prove as visionary and fallacious as the government of Congress," evidently meaning the then existing Congress of the old Confederation.

Without descending to particulars, it may be safely asserted that the power to make war against a State is at variance with the whole spirit and intent of the Constitution. Suppose such a war should result in the conquest of a State; how are we to govern it afterwards? Shall we hold it as a province and govern it by despotic power? In the nature of things, we could not by physical force control the will of the people and compel them to elect Senators and Representatives to Congress and to perform all the other duties depending upon their own volition and required from the free citizens of a free State as a constituent member of the Confederacy.

But if we possessed this power, would it be wise to exercise it under existing circumstances? The object would doubtless be to preserve the Union. War would not only present the most effectual means of destroying it, but would vanish all hope of its peaceable reconstruction. Besides, in the fraternal conflict a vast amount of blood and treasure would be expended, rendering future reconciliation between the States impossible. In the meantime, who can foretell what would be the sufferings and privations of the people during its existence?

The fact is that our Union rests upon public opinion, and can never be cemented by the blood of its citizens shed in civil war. If it can not live in the affections of the people, it must one day perish. Congress possesses many means of preserving it by conciliation, but the sword was not placed in their hand to preserve it by force.

But may I be permitted solemnly to invoke my countrymen to pause and deliberate before they determine to destroy this the grandest temple which has ever been dedicated to human freedom since the world began? It has been consecrated by the blood of our fathers, by the glories of the past, and by the hopes of the future. The Union has already made us the most prosperous, and ere long will, if preserved, render us the most powerful, nation on the face of the earth. In every foreign region of the globe the title of American citizen is held in the highest respect, and when pronounced in a foreign land it causes the hearts of our countrymen to swell with honest pride. Surely when we reach the brink of the yawning abyss we shall recoil with horror from the last fatal plunge.

By such a dread catastrophe the hopes of the friends of freedom throughout the world would be destroyed, and a long night of leaden despotism would enshroud the nations. Our example for more than eighty years would not only be lost, but it would be quoted as a conclusive proof that man is unfit for self-government.

It is not every wrong-nay, it is not every grievous wrong-which can justify a resort to such a fearful alternative. This ought to be the last desperate remedy of a despairing people, after every other constitutional means of conciliation had been exhausted. We should reflect that under this free Government there is an incessant ebb and flow in public opinion. The slavery question, like everything human, will have its day. I firmly believe that it has reached and passed the culminating point. But if in the midst of the existing excitement the Union shall perish, the evil may then become irreparable.

Congress can contribute much to avert it by proposing and recommending to the legislatures of the several States the remedy for existing evils which the Constitution has itself provided for its own preservation. This has been tried at different critical periods of our history, and always with eminent success. It is to be found in the fifth article, providing for its own amendment. Under this article amendments have been proposed by two-thirds of both Houses of Congress, and have been "ratified by the legislatures of three-fourths of the several States," and have consequently become parts of the Constitution. To this process the country is indebted for the clause prohibiting Congress from passing any law respecting an establishment of religion or abridging the freedom of speech or of the press or of the right of petition. To this we are also indebted for the bill of rights which secures the people against any abuse of power by the Federal Government. Such were the apprehensions justly entertained by the friends of State rights at that period as to have rendered it extremely doubtful whether the Constitution could have long survived without those amendments.

Again the Constitution was amended by the same process, after the election of President Jefferson by the House of Representatives, in February, 1803. This amendment was rendered necessary to prevent a recurrence of the dangers which had seriously threatened the existence of the Government during the pendency of that election. The article for its own amendment was intended to secure the amicable adjustment of conflicting constitutional questions like the present which might arise between the governments of the States and that of the United States. This appears from contemporaneous history. In this connection I shall merely call attention to a few sentences in Mr. Madison's justly celebrated report, in 1799, to the legislature of Virginia. In this he ably and conclusively defended the resolutions of the preceding legislature against the strictures of several other State legislatures. These were mainly rounded upon the protest of the Virginia legislature against the "alien and sedition acts," as "palpable and alarming infractions of the Constitution." In pointing out the peaceful and constitutional remedies-and he referred to none other-to which the States were authorized to resort on such occasions, he concludes by saying that-

The legislatures of the States might have made a direct representation to Congress with a view to obtain a rescinding of the two offensive acts, or they might have represented to their respective Senators in Congress their wish that two-thirds thereof would propose an explanatory amendment to the Constitution; or two-thirds of themselves, if such had been their option, might by an application to Congress have obtained a convention for the same object.

This is the very course which I earnestly recommend in order to obtain an "explanatory amendment" of the Constitution on the subject of slavery. This might originate with Congress or the State legislatures, as may be deemed most advisable to attain the object. The explanatory amendment might be confined to the final settlement of the true construction of the Constitution on three special points:

1. An express recognition of the right of property in slaves in the States where it now exists or may hereafter exist.

2. The duty of protecting this right in all the common Territories throughout their Territorial existence, and until they shall be admitted as

17

States into the Union, with or without slavery, as their constitutions may prescribe.

3. A like recognition of the right of the master to have his slave who has escaped from one State to another restored and "delivered up" to him, and of the validity of the fugitive-slave law enacted for this purpose, together with a declaration that all State laws impairing or defeating this right are violations of the Constitution, and are consequently null and void. It may be objected that this construction of the Constitution has already been settled by the Supreme Court of the United States, and what more ought to be required? The answer is that a very large proportion of the people of the United States still contest the correctness of this decision, and never will cease from agitation and admit its binding force until clearly established by the people of the several States in their sovereign character. Such an explanatory amendment would, it is believed, forever terminate the existing dissensions, and restore peace and harmony among the States.

It ought not to be doubted that such an appeal to the arbitrament established by the Constitution itself would be received with favor by all the States of the Confederacy. In any event, it ought to be tried in a spirit of conciliation before any of these States shall separate themselves from the Union.

When I entered upon the duties of the Presidential office, the aspect neither of our foreign nor domestic affairs was at all satisfactory. We were involved in dangerous complications with several nations, and two of our Territories were in a state of revolution against the Government. A restoration of the African slave trade had numerous and powerful advocates. Unlawful military expeditions were countenanced by many of our citizens, and were suffered, in defiance of the efforts of the Government, to escape from our shores for the purpose of making war upon the offending people of neighboring republics with whom we were at peace. In addition to these and other difficulties, we experienced a revulsion in monetary affairs soon after my advent to power of unexampled severity and of ruinous consequences to all the great interests of the country. When we take a retrospect of what was then our condition and contrast this with its material prosperity at the time of the late Presidential election, we have abundant reason to return our grateful thanks to that merciful Providence which has never forsaken us as a nation in all our past trials.

Our relations with Great Britain are of the most friendly character. Since the commencement of my Administration the two dangerous questions arising from the Clayton and Bulwer treaty and from the right of search claimed by the British Government have been amicably and honorably adjusted.

The discordant constructions of the Clayton and Bulwer treaty between the two Governments, which at different periods of the discussion bore a threatening aspect, have resulted in a final settlement entirely satisfactory to this Government. In my last annual message I informed Congress that the British Government had not then "completed treaty arrangements with the Republics of Honduras and Nicaragua in pursuance of the understanding between the two Governments. It is, nevertheless, confidently expected that this good work will ere long be accomplished." This confident expectation has since been fulfilled. Her Britannic Majesty concluded a treaty with Honduras on the 28th November, 1859, and with Nicaragua on the 28th August, 1860, relinquishing the Mosquito protectorate. Besides, by the former the Bay Islands are recognized as a part of the Republic of Honduras. It may be observed that the stipulations of these treaties conform in every "important particular to the amendments adopted by the Senate of the United States to the treaty concluded at London on the 17th October, 1856, between the two Governments. It will be recollected that this treaty was rejected by the British Government because of its objection to the just and important amendment of the Senate to the article relating to Ruatan and the other islands in the Bay of Honduras.

It must be a source of sincere satisfaction to all classes of our fellow-citizens, and especially to those engaged in foreign commerce, that the claim on the part of Great Britain forcibly to visit and search American merchant vessels on the high seas in time of peace has been abandoned. This was by far the most dangerous question to the peace of the two countries which has existed since the War of 1812. Whilst it remained open they might at any moment have been precipitated into a war. This was rendered manifest by the exasperated state of public feeling throughout our entire country produced by the forcible search of American merchant vessels by British cruisers on the coast of Cuba in the spring of 1858. The American people hailed with general acclaim the orders of the Secretary of the Navy to our naval force in the Gulf of Mexico "to protect all vessels of the United States on the high seas from search or detention by the vessels of war of any other nation." These orders might have produced an immediate collision between the naval forces of the two countries. This was most fortunately prevented by an appeal to the justice of Great Britain and to the law of nations as expounded by her own most eminent jurists.

The only question of any importance which still remains open is the disputed title between the two Governments to the island of San Juan, in the vicinity of Washington Territory. As this question is still under negotiation, it is not deemed advisable at the present moment to make any other allusion to the subject.

The recent visit of the Prince of Wales, in a private character, to the people of this country has proved to be a most auspicious event. In its consequences it can not fail to increase the kindred and kindly feelings which I trust may ever actuate the Government and people of both

19

countries in their political and social intercourse with each other.

With France, our ancient and powerful ally, our relations continue to be of the most friendly character. A decision has recently been made by a French judicial tribunal, with the approbation of the Imperial Government, which can not fail to foster the sentiments of mutual regard that have so long existed between the two countries. Under the French law no person can serve in the armies of France unless he be a French citizen. The law of France recognizing the natural right of expatriation, it follows as a necessary consequence that a Frenchman by the fact of having become a citizen of the United States has changed his allegiance and has lost his native character. He can not therefore be compelled to serve in the French armies in case he should return to his native country. These principles were announced in 1852 by the French minister of war and in two late cases have been confirmed by the French judiciary. In these, two natives of France have been discharged from the French army because they had become American citizens. To employ the language of our present minister to France, who has rendered good service on this occasion. "I do not think our French naturalized fellow-citizens will hereafter experience much annoyance on this subject."

I venture to predict that the time is not far distant when the other continental powers will adopt the same wise and just policy which has done so much honor to the enlightened Government of the Emperor. In any event, our Government is bound to protect the rights of our naturalized citizens everywhere to the same extent as though they had drawn their first breath in this country. We can recognize no distinction between our native and naturalized citizens.

Between the great Empire of Russia and the United States the mutual friendship and regard which has so long existed still continues to prevail, and if possible to increase. Indeed, our relations with that Empire are all that we could desire. Our relations with Spain are now of a more complicated, though less dangerous, character than they have been for many years. Our citizens have long held and continue to hold numerous claims against the Spanish Government. These had been ably urged for a series of years by our successive diplomatic representatives at Madrid, but without obtaining redress. The Spanish Government finally agreed to institute a joint commission for the adjustment of these claims, and on the 5th day of March, 1860, concluded a convention for this purpose with our present minister at Madrid.

Under this convention what have been denominated the "Cuban claims," amounting to $128,635.54, in which more than 100 of our fellow-citizens are interested, were recognized, and the Spanish Government agreed to pay $100,000 of this amount "within three months following the exchange of ratifications." The payment of the remaining $28,635.54 was to await the decision of the commissioners for or against the Amistad claim; but in any event the balance was to be paid to the claimants either by Spain or the United States. These terms, I have every reason to know, are highly satisfactory to the holders of the Cuban claims. Indeed, they have made a formal offer authorizing the State Department to settle these claims and to deduct the amount of the Amistad claim from the sums which they are entitled to receive from Spain. This offer, of course, can not be accepted. All other claims of citizens of the United States against Spain, or the subjects of the Queen of Spain against the United States, including the Amistad claim, were by this convention referred to a board of commissioners in the usual form. Neither the validity of the Amistad claim nor of any other claim against either party, with the single exception of the Cuban claims, was recognized by the convention. Indeed, the Spanish Government did not insist that the validity of the Amistad claim should be thus recognized, notwithstanding its payment had been recommended to Congress by two of my predecessors, as well as by myself, and an appropriation for that purpose had passed the Senate of the United States.

They were content that it should be submitted to the board for examination and decision like the other claims. Both Governments were bound respectively to pay the amounts awarded to the several claimants "at such times and places as may be fixed by and according to the tenor of said awards."

I transmitted this convention to the Senate for their constitutional action on the 3d of May, 1860, and on the 27th of the succeeding June they determined that they would "not advise and consent" to its ratification.

These proceedings place our relations with Spain in an awkward and embarrassing position. It is more than probable that the final adjustment of these claims will devolve upon my successor.

I reiterate the recommendation contained in my annual message of December, 1858, and repeated in that of December, 1859, in favor of the acquisition of Cuba from Spain by fair purchase. I firmly believe that such an acquisition would contribute essentially to the well-being and prosperity of both countries in all future time, as well as prove the certain means of immediately abolishing the African slave trade throughout the world. I would not repeat this recommendation upon the present occasion if I believed that the transfer of Cuba to the United States upon conditions highly favorable to Spain could justly tarnish the national honor of the proud and ancient Spanish monarchy. Surely no person ever attributed to the first Napoleon a disregard of the national honor of France for transferring Louisiana to the United States for a fair equivalent, both in money and commercial advantages.

With the Emperor of Austria and the remaining continental powers of Europe, including that of the Sultan, our relations continue to be of the most friendly character.

The friendly and peaceful policy pursued by the Government of the United States toward the Empire of China has produced the most satisfactory results. The treaty of Tien-tsin of the 18th June, 1858, has been faithfully observed by the Chinese authorities. The convention of the 8th November, 1858, supplementary to this treaty, for the adjustment and satisfaction of the claims of our citizens on China referred to in my last annual message, has been already carried into effect so far as this was practicable. Under this convention the sum of 500,000 taels, equal to about $700,000, was stipulated to be paid in satisfaction of the claims of American citizens out of the one-fifth of the receipts for tonnage, import, and export duties on American vessels at the ports of Canton, Shanghai, and Fuchau, and it was "agreed that this amount shall be in full liquidation of all claims of American citizens at the various ports to this date." Debentures for this amount, to wit, 300,000 taels for Canton, 100,000 for Shanghai, and 100,000 for Fuchau, were delivered, according to the terms of the convention, by the respective Chinese collectors of the customs of these ports to the agent selected by our minister to receive the same. Since that time the claims of our citizens have been adjusted by the board of commissioners appointed for that purpose under the act of March 3, 1859, and their awards, which proved satisfactory to the claimants, have been approved by our minister. In the aggregate they amount to the sum of $498,694.78. The claimants have already received a large proportion of the sums awarded to them out of the fund provided, and it is confidently expected that the remainder will ere long be entirely paid. After the awards shall have been satisfied there will remain a surplus of more than $200,000 at the disposition of Congress. As this will, in equity, belong to the Chinese Government, would not justice require its appropriation to some benevolent object in which the Chinese may be specially interested?

Our minister to China, in obedience to his instructions, has remained perfectly neutral in the war between Great Britain and France and the Chinese Empire, although, in conjunction with the Russian minister, he was ever ready and willing, had the opportunity offered, to employ his good offices in restoring peace between the parties. It is but an act of simple justice, both to our present minister and his predecessor, to state that they have proved fully equal to the delicate, trying, and responsible positions in which they have on different occasions been placed.

The ratifications of the treaty with Japan concluded at Yeddo on the 29th July, 1858, were exchanged at Washington on the 22d May last, and the treaty itself was proclaimed on the succeeding day. There is good reason to expect that under its protection and influence our trade and intercourse with that distant and interesting people will rapidly increase.

The ratifications of the treaty were exchanged with unusual solemnity. For this purpose the Tycoon had accredited three of his most distinguished subjects as envoys extraordinary and ministers plenipotentiary, who were received and treated with marked distinction and kindness, both by the Government and people of the United States. There is every reason to believe that they have returned to their native land entirely satisfied with their visit and inspired by the most friendly feelings for our country. Let us ardently hope, in the language of the treaty itself, that "there shall henceforward be perpetual peace and friendship between the United States of America and His Majesty the Tycoon of Japan and his successors."

With the wise, conservative, and liberal Government of the Empire of Brazil our relations continue to be of the most amicable character.

The exchange of the ratifications of the convention with the Republic of New Granada signed at Washington on the 10th of September, 1857, has been long delayed from accidental causes for which neither party is censurable. These ratifications were duly exchanged in this city on the 5th of November last. Thus has a controversy been amicably terminated which had become so serious at the period of my inauguration as to require me, on the 17th of April, 1857, to direct our minister to demand his passports and return to the United States.

Under this convention the Government of New Granada has specially acknowledged itself to be responsible to our citizens "for damages which were caused by the riot at Panama on the 15th April, 1856." These claims, together with other claims of our citizens which had been long urged in vain, are referred for adjustment to a board of commissioners. I submit a copy of the convention to Congress, and recommend the legislation necessary to carry it into effect.

Persevering efforts have been made for the adjustment of the claims of American citizens against the Government of Costa Rica, and I am happy to inform you that these have finally prevailed. A convention was signed at the city of San Jose on the 2d July last, between the minister resident of the United States in Costa Rica and the plenipotentiaries of that Republic, referring these claims to a board of commissioners and providing for the payment of their awards. This convention will be submitted immediately to the Senate for their constitutional action.

The claims of our citizens upon the Republic of Nicaragua have not yet been provided for by treaty, although diligent efforts for this purpose have been made by our minister resident to that Republic. These are still continued, with a fair prospect of success.

Our relations with Mexico remain in a most unsatisfactory condition. In my last two annual messages I discussed extensively the subject of these relations, and do not now propose to repeat at length the facts and arguments then presented. They proved conclusively that our citizens residing in Mexico and our merchants trading thereto had suffered a series of wrongs and outrages such as we have never patiently borne from any other nation. For these our successive ministers, invoking the faith of treaties, had in the name of their country persistently demanded redress and indemnification, but without the slightest effect. Indeed, so confident had the Mexican authorities become of our patient endurance that they universally believed they might commit these outrages upon American citizens with absolute impunity. Thus wrote our minister in 1856, and expressed the opinion that "nothing but a manifestation of the power of the Government and of its purpose to punish these wrongs will avail."

Afterwards, in 1857, came the adoption of a new constitution for Mexico, the election of a President and Congress under its provisions, and the inauguration of the President. Within one short month, however, this President was expelled from the capital by a rebellion in the army, and the supreme power of the Republic was assigned to General Zuloaga. This usurper was in his turn soon compelled to retire and give place to General Miramon.

Under the constitution which had thus been adopted Senor Juarez, as chief justice of the supreme court, became the lawful President of the Republic, and it was for the maintenance of the constitution and his authority derived from it that the civil war commenced and still continues to be prosecuted.

Throughout the year 1858 the constitutional party grew stronger and stronger. In the previous history of Mexico a successful military revolution at the capital had almost universally been the signal for submission throughout the Republic. Not so on the present occasion. A majority of the citizens persistently sustained the constitutional Government. When this was recognized, in April, 1859, by the Government of the United States, its authority extended over a large majority of the Mexican States and people, including Vera Cruz and all the other important seaports of the Republic. From that period our commerce with Mexico began to revive, and the constitutional Government has afforded it all the protection in its power.

Meanwhile the Government of Miramon still held sway at the capital and over the surrounding country, and continued its outrages against the few American citizens who still had the courage to remain within its power. To cap the climax, after the battle of Tacubaya, in April, 1859, General Marquez ordered three citizens of the United States, two of them physicians, to be seized in the hospital at that place, taken out and shot, without crime and without trial. This was done, notwithstanding our unfortunate countrymen were at the moment engaged in the holy cause of affording relief to the soldiers of both parties who had been wounded in the battle, without making any distinction between them.

The time had arrived, in my opinion, when this Government was bound to exert its power to avenge and redress the wrongs of our citizens and to afford them protection in Mexico. The interposing obstacle was that the portion of the country under the sway of Miramon could not be reached without passing over territory under the jurisdiction of the constitutional Government. Under these circumstances I deemed it my duty to recommend to Congress in my last annual message the employment of a sufficient military force to penetrate into the interior, where the Government of Miramon was to be found, with or, if need be, without the consent of the Juarez Government, though it was not doubted that this consent could be obtained. Never have I had a clearer conviction on any subject than of the justice as well as wisdom of such a policy. No other alternative was left except the entire abandonment of our fellow-citizens who had gone to Mexico under the faith of treaties to the systematic injustice, cruelty, and oppression of Miramon's Government. Besides, it is almost certain that the simple authority to employ this force would of itself have accomplished all our objects without striking a single blow. The constitutional Government would then ere this have been established at the City of Mexico, and would have been ready and willing to the extent of its ability to do us justice.

In addition-and I deem this a most important consideration-European Governments would have been deprived of all pretext to interfere in the territorial and domestic concerns of Mexico. We should thus have been relieved from the obligation of resisting, even by force should this become necessary, any attempt by these Governments to deprive our neighboring Republic of portions of her territory-a duty from which we could not shrink without abandoning the traditional and established policy of the American people. I am happy to observe that, firmly relying upon the justice and good faith of these Governments, there is no present danger that such a contingency will happen.

Having discovered that my recommendations would not be sustained by Congress, the next alternative was to accomplish in some degree, if possible, the same objects by treaty stipulations with the constitutional Government. Such treaties were accordingly concluded by our late able and excellent minister to Mexico, and on the 4th of January last were submitted to the Senate for ratification. As these have not yet received the final action of that body, it would be improper for me to present a detailed statement of their provisions. Still, I may be permitted to express the opinion in advance that they are calculated to promote the agricultural, manufacturing, and commercial interests of the country and to secure our just influence with an adjoining Republic as to whose fortunes and fate we can never feel indifferent, whilst at the same time they provide for the payment of a considerable amount toward the satisfaction of the claims of our injured fellow-citizens.

At the period of my inauguration I was confronted in Kansas by a revolutionary government existing under what is called the "Topeka constitution." Its avowed object was to subdue the Territorial government by force and to inaugurate what was called the "Topeka government" in its stead. To accomplish this object an extensive military organization was formed, and its command intrusted to the most violent revolutionary leaders. Under these circumstances it became my imperative duty to exert the whole constitutional power of the Executive to prevent the flames of civil war from again raging in Kansas, which in the excited state of the public mind, both North and South, might have extended into the neighboring States. The hostile parties in Kansas had been inflamed against each other by emissaries both from the North and the South to a degree of malignity without parallel in our history. To prevent actual collision and to assist the civil magistrates in enforcing the laws, a strong detachment of the Army was stationed in the Territory, ready to aid the marshal and his deputies when lawfully called upon as a posse comitatus in the execution of civil and criminal process. Still, the troubles in Kansas could not have been permanently settled without an election by the people.

The ballot box is the surest arbiter of disputes among freemen. Under this conviction every proper effort was employed to induce the hostile parties to vote at the election of delegates to frame a State constitution, and afterwards at the election to decide whether Kansas should be a slave or free State.

The insurgent party refused to vote at either, lest this might be considered a recognition on their part of the Territorial government established by Congress. A better spirit, however, seemed soon after to prevail, and the two parties met face to face at the third election, held on the first Monday of January, 1858, for members of the legislature and State officers under the Lecompton constitution. The result was the triumph of the antislavery party at the polls. This decision of the ballot box proved clearly that this party were in the majority, and removed the danger of civil war. From that time we have heard little or nothing of the Topeka government, and all serious danger of revolutionary troubles in Kansas was then at an end.

The Lecompton constitution, which had been thus recognized at this State election by the votes of both political parties in Kansas, was transmitted to me with the request that I should present it to Congress. This I could not have refused to do without violating my clearest and strongest convictions of duty. The constitution and all the proceedings which preceded and followed its formation were fair and regular on their face. I then believed, and experience has proved, that the interests of the people of Kansas would have been best consulted by its admission as a State into the Union, especially as the majority within a brief period could have amended the constitution according to their will and pleasure. If fraud existed in all or any of these proceedings, it was not for the President but for Congress to investigate and determine the question of fraud and what ought to be its consequences. If at the first two elections the majority refused to vote, it can not be pretended that this refusal to exercise the elective franchise could invalidate an election fairly held under lawful authority, even if they had not subsequently voted at the third election. It is true that the whole constitution had not been submitted to the people, as I always desired; but the precedents are numerous of the admission of States into the Union without such submission. It would not comport with my present purpose to review the proceedings of Congress upon the Lecompton constitution. It is sufficient to observe that their final action has removed the last vestige of serious revolutionary troubles. The desperate hand recently assembled under a notorious outlaw in the southern portion of the Territory to resist the execution of the laws and to plunder peaceful citizens will, I doubt not be speedily subdued and brought to justice.

Had I treated the Lecompton constitution as a nullity and refused to transmit it to Congress, it is not difficult to imagine, whilst recalling the position of the country at that moment, what would have been the disastrous consequences, both in and out of the Territory, from such a dereliction of duty on the part of the Executive.

Peace has also been restored within the Territory of Utah, which at the commencement of my Administration was in a state of open rebellion. This was the more dangerous, as the people, animated by a fanatical spirit and intrenched within their distant mountain fastnesses, might have made a long and formidable resistance. Cost what it might, it was necessary to bring them into subjection to the Constitution and the laws. Sound policy, therefore, as well as humanity, required that this object should if possible be accomplished without the effusion of blood. This could only be effected by sending a military force into the Territory sufficiently strong to convince the people that resistance would be hopeless, and at the same time to offer them a pardon for past offenses on condition of immediate submission to the Government. This policy was pursued with eminent success, and the only cause for regret is the heavy expenditure required to march a large detachment of the Army to that remote region and to furnish it subsistence. Utah is now comparatively peaceful and quiet, and the military force has been withdrawn, except that portion of it necessary to keep the Indians in check and to protect the emigrant trains on their way to our Pacific possessions.

In my first annual message I promised to employ my best exertions in cooperation with Congress to reduce the expenditures of the Government within the limits of a wise and judicious economy. An overflowing Treasury had produced habits of prodigality and extravagance which could only be gradually corrected. The work required both time and patience. I applied myself diligently to this task from the beginning and was aided by the able and energetic efforts of the heads of the different Executive Departments.

The result of our labors in this good cause did not appear in the sum total of our expenditures for the first two years, mainly in consequence of the extraordinary expenditure necessarily incurred in the Utah expedition and the very large amount of the contingent expenses of Congress during this period. These greatly exceeded the pay and mileage of the members. For the year ending June 30, 1858, whilst the pay and mileage amounted to $1,490,214, the contingent expenses rose to $2,093,309.79; and for the year ending June 30, 1859, whilst the pay and mileage amounted to $859,093.66, the contingent expenses amounted to $1,431,565.78. I am happy, however, to be able to inform you that during the last fiscal year, ending June 30, 1860, the total expenditures of the Government in all its branches-legislative, executive, and judicial-exclusive of the public debt, were reduced to the sum of $55,402,465.46. This conclusively appears from the books of the Treasury. In the year ending June 30, 1858, the total expenditure, exclusive of the public debt, amounted to $71,901,129.77, and that for the year ending June 30, 1859, to $66,346,226.13. Whilst the books of the Treasury show an actual expenditure of $59,848,474.72 for the year ending June 30, 1860, including $1,040,667.71 for the contingent expenses of Congress, there must be deducted from this amount the sum of $4,296,009.26, with the interest upon it of $150,000, appropriated by the act of February 15, 1860, "for the purpose of supplying the deficiency in the revenues and defraying the expenses of the Post-Office Department for the year ending June 30, 1859." This sum therefore justly chargeable to the year 1859, must be deducted from the sum of $59,848,474.72 in order to ascertain the expenditure for the year ending June 30, 1860, which leaves a balance for the expenditures of that year of $55,402,465.46. The interest on the public debt, including Treasury notes, for the same fiscal year, ending June 30, 1860, amounted to $3,177,314.62, which, added to the above sum of $55,402,465.46, makes the aggregate of $58,579,780.08.

It ought in justice to be observed that several of the estimates from the Departments for the year ending June 30, 1860, were reduced by Congress below what was and still is deemed compatible with the public interest. Allowing a liberal margin of $2,500,000 for this reduction and for other causes, it may be safely asserted that the sum of $61,000,000, or, at the most, $62,000,000, is amply sufficient to administer the Government and to pay the interest on the public debt, unless contingent events should hereafter render extraordinary expenditures necessary.

This result has been attained in a considerable degree by the care exercised by the appropriate Departments in entering into public contracts. I have myself never interfered with the award of any such contract, except in a single case, with the Colonization Society, deeming it advisable to cast the whole responsibility in each case on the proper head of the Department, with the general instruction that these contracts should always be given to the lowest and best bidder. It has ever been my opinion that public contracts are not a legitimate source of patronage to be conferred upon personal or political favorites, but that in all such cases a public officer is bound to act for the Government as a prudent individual would act for himself.

It is with great satisfaction I communicate the fact that since the date of my last annual message not a single slave has been imported into the United States in violation of the laws prohibiting the African slave trade. This statement is rounded upon a thorough examination and investigation of the subject. Indeed, the spirit which prevailed some time since among a portion of our fellow-citizens in favor of this trade seems to have entirely subsided.

I also congratulate you upon the public sentiment which now exists against the crime of setting on foot military expeditions within the limits of the United States to proceed from thence and make war upon the people of unoffending States with whom we are at peace. In this respect a happy change has been effected since the commencement of my Administration. It surely ought to be the prayer of every Christian and patriot that such expeditions may never again receive countenance in our country or depart from our shores.

It would be a useless repetition to do more than refer with earnest commendation to my former recommendations in favor of the Pacific railroad; of the grant of power to the President to employ the naval force in the vicinity for the protection of the lives and property of our fellow-citizens passing in transit over the different Central American routes against sudden and lawless outbreaks and depredations, and also to protect American merchant vessels, their crews and cargoes, against violent and unlawful seizure and confiscation in the ports of Mexico and the South American Republics when these may be in a disturbed and revolutionary condition. It is my settled conviction that without such a power we do not afford that protection to those engaged in the commerce of the country which they have a right to demand.

I again recommend to Congress the passage of a law, in pursuance of the provisions of the Constitution, appointing a day certain previous to the 4th March in each year of an odd number for the election of Representatives throughout all the States. A similar power has already been exercised, with general approbation, in the appointment of the same day throughout the Union for holding the election of electors for President and Vice-President of the United States. My attention was earnestly directed to this subject from the fact that the Thirty-fifth Congress terminated on the 3d March, 1859, without making the necessary appropriation for the service of the Post-Office Department. I was then forced to consider the best remedy for this omission, and an immediate call of the present Congress was the natural resort. Upon inquiry, however, I ascertained that fifteen out of the thirty-three States composing the Confederacy were without Representatives, and that consequently these fifteen States would be disfranchised by such a call. These fifteen States will be in the same condition on the 4th March next. Ten of them can not elect Representatives, according to existing State laws, until different periods, extending from the beginning of August next until the months of October and November. In my last message I gave warning that in a time of sudden and alarming danger the salvation of our institutions might depend upon the power of the President immediately to assemble a full Congress to meet the emergency.

It is now quite evident that the financial necessities of the Government will require a modification of the tariff during your present session for the purpose of increasing the revenue. In this aspect, I desire to reiterate the recommendation contained in my last two annual messages in favor of imposing specific instead of ad valorem duties on all imported articles to which these can be properly applied. From long observation and experience I am convinced that specific duties are necessary, both to protect the revenue and to secure to our manufacturing interests that amount of incidental encouragement which unavoidably results from a revenue tariff.

As an abstract proposition it may be admitted that ad valorem duties would in theory be the most just and equal. But if the experience of this and of all other commercial nations has demonstrated that such duties can not be assessed and collected without great frauds upon the revenue, then it is the part of wisdom to resort to specific duties. Indeed, from the very nature of an ad valorem duty this must be the result. Under it the inevitable consequence is that foreign goods will be entered at less than their true value. The Treasury will therefore lose the duty on the difference between their real and fictitious value, and to this extent we are defrauded.

The temptations which ad valorem duties present to a dishonest importer are irresistible. His object is to pass his goods through the custom-house at the very lowest valuation necessary to save them from confiscation. In this he too often succeeds in spite of the vigilance of the revenue officers. Hence the resort to false invoices, one for the purchaser and another for the custom-house, and to other expedients to defraud the Government. The honest importer produces his invoice to the collector, stating the actual price at which he purchased the articles abroad. Not so the dishonest importer and the agent of the foreign manufacturer. And here it may be observed that a very large proportion of the manufactures imported from abroad are consigned for sale to commission merchants, who are mere agents employed by the manufacturers. In such cases no actual sale has been made to fix their value. The foreign manufacturer, if he be dishonest, prepares an invoice of the goods, not at their actual value, but at the very lowest rate necessary to escape detection. In this manner the dishonest importer and the foreign manufacturer enjoy a decided advantage over the honest merchant. They are thus enabled to undersell the fair trader and drive him from the market. In fact the operation of this system has already driven from the pursuits of honorable commerce many of that class of regular and conscientious merchants whose character throughout the world is the pride of our country.

The remedy for these evils is to be found in specific duties, so far as this may be practicable. They dispense with any inquiry at the custom-house into the actual cost or value of the article, and it pays the precise amount of duty previously fixed by law. They present no temptations to the appraisers of foreign goods, who receive but small salaries, and might by undervaluation in a few cases render themselves independent.

Besides, specific duties best conform to the requisition in the Constitution that "no preference shall be given by any regulation of commerce or revenue to the ports of one State over those of another." Under our ad valorem system such preferences are to some extent inevitable, and complaints have often been made that the spirit of this provision has been violated by a lower appraisement of the same articles at one port than at another.

An impression strangely enough prevails to some extent that specific duties are necessarily protective duties. Nothing can be more fallacious. Great Britain glories in free trade, and yet her whole revenue from imports is at the present moment collected under a system of specific duties. It is a striking fact in this connection that in the commercial treaty of January 23, 1860, between France and England one of the articles provides that the ad valorem duties which it imposes shall be converted into specific duties within six months from its date, and these are to be ascertained by making an average of the prices for six months previous to that time. The reverse of the propositions would be nearer to the truth, because a much larger amount of revenue would be collected by merely converting the ad valorem duties of a tariff into equivalent specific duties. To this extent the revenue would be increased, and in the same proportion the specific duty might be diminished.

Specific duties would secure to the American manufacturer the incidental protection to which he is fairly entitled under a revenue tariff, and to this surely no person would object. The framers of the existing tariff have gone further, and in a liberal spirit have discriminated in favor of large and useful branches of our manufactures, not by raising the rate of duty upon the importation of similar articles from abroad, but, what is the same in effect, by admitting articles free of duty which enter into the composition of their fabrics.

Under the present system it has been often truly remarked that this incidental protection decreases when the manufacturer needs it most and increases when he needs it least, and constitutes a sliding scale which always operates against him. The revenues of the country are subject to similar fluctuations. Instead of approaching a steady standard, as would be the case under a system of specific duties, they sink and rise with the sinking and rising prices of articles in foreign countries. It would not be difficult for Congress to arrange a system of specific duties which would afford additional stability both to our revenue and our manufactures and without injury or injustice to any interest of the country. This might be accomplished by ascertaining the average value of any given article for a series of years at the place of exportation and by simply converting the rate of ad valorem duty upon it which might be deemed necessary for revenue purposes into the form of a specific duty. Such an arrangement could not injure the consumer. If he should pay a greater amount of duty one year, this would be counterbalanced by a lesser amount the next, and in the end the aggregate would be the same.

I desire to call your immediate attention to the present condition of the Treasury, so ably and clearly presented by the Secretary in his report to Congress, and to recommend that measures be promptly adopted to enable it to discharge its pressing obligations. The other recommendations of the report are well worthy of your favorable consideration.

I herewith transmit to Congress the reports of the Secretaries of War, of the Navy, of the Interior, and of the Postmaster-General. The recommendations and suggestions which they contain are highly valuable and deserve your careful attention.

The report of the Postmaster-General details the circumstances under which Cornelius Vanderbilt, on my request, agreed in the month of July last to carry the ocean mails between our Atlantic and Pacific coasts. Had he not thus acted this important intercommunication must have been suspended, at least for a season. The Postmaster-General had no power to make him any other compensation than the postages on the mail matter which he might carry. It was known at the time that these postages would fall far short of an adequate compensation, as well as of the sum which the same service had previously cost the Government. Mr. Vanderbilt, in a commendable spirit, was willing to rely upon the justice of Congress to make up the deficiency, and I therefore recommend that an appropriation may be granted for this purpose.

I should do great injustice to the Attorney-General were I to omit the mention of his distinguished services in the measures adopted and prosecuted by him for the defense of the Government against numerous and unfounded claims to land in California purporting to have been made by the Mexican Government previous to the treaty of cession. The successful opposition to these claims has saved the United States public property worth many millions of dollars and to individuals holding title under them to at least an equal amount.

It has been represented to me from sources which I deem reliable that the inhabitants in several portions of Kansas have been reduced nearly to a state of starvation on account of the almost total failure of their crops, whilst the harvests in every other portion of the country have been abundant. The prospect before them for the approaching winter is well calculated to enlist the sympathies of every heart. The destitution appears to be so general that it can not be relieved by private contributions, and they are in such indigent circumstances as to be unable to purchase the necessaries of life for themselves. I refer the subject to Congress. If any constitutional measure for their relief can be devised, I would recommend its adoption.

I cordially commend to your favorable regard the interests of the people of this District. They are eminently entitled to your consideration, especially since, unlike the people of the States, they can appeal to no government except that of the Union.

www.ingramcontent.com/pod-product-compliance
Lightning Source LLC
Chambersburg PA
CBHW070522290526
45790CB00003B/1265